with

AMERICAN HUMANE

Protecting Children & Animals Since 1877

SERVICE DOG HEROES

Titles in the Amazing Working Dogs with American Humane Series

FIRE DOG HEROES
ISBN-13: 978-0-7660-3202-6

GUIDE DOG HEROES
ISBN-13: 978-0-7660-3198-2

POLICE DOG HEROES
ISBN-13: 978-0-7660-3197-5

SEARCH AND RESCUE DOG HEROES
ISBN-13: 978-0-7660-3201-9

SERVICE DOG HEROES
ISBN-13: 978-0-7660-3199-9

THERAPY DOG HEROES
ISBN-13: 978-0-7660-3200-2

AMAZING WORKING DOGS with

AMERICAN HUMANE
Protecting Children & Animals Since 1877

SERVICE DOG HEROES

Linda
Bozzo

Bailey Books
an imprint of
Enslow Publishers, Inc.
40 Industrial Road
Box 398
Berkeley Heights, NJ 07922
USA
http://www.enslow.com

This book dedicated to Jacqueline Rotteveel and her loving dog, Kazi, for inviting me into their home and for teaching me so much more than what's written in this book.

Founded in 1877, the American Humane Association is the only national organization dedicated to protecting both children and animals. Through a network of child and animal protection agencies and individuals, American Humane develops policies, legislation, curricula, and training programs—and takes action—to protect children and animals from abuse, neglect, and exploitation. To learn how you can support American Humane's vision of a nation where no child or animal will ever be a victim of abuse or neglect, visit www.americanhumane.org, phone (303) 792-9900, or write to the American Humane Association at 63 Inverness Drive East, Englewood, Colorado, 80112-5117.

AMERICAN HUMAN

Protecting Children & Animals Since 1877

Bailey Books, an imprint of Enslow Publishers, Inc.

Copyright © 2011 by Enslow Publishers, Inc.

Library of Congress Cataloging-in-Publication Data

Bozzo, Linda.

   Service dog heroes / Linda Bozzo.

      p. cm. — (Amazing working dogs with American humane)

   Includes bibliographical references and index.

   Summary: "The text opens with a true story of a service dog, and then it explains the history of service dog and the training methods used to transform an ordinary dog into a canine hero"—Provided by publisher.

   ISBN 978-0-7660-3199-9

   1. Service dogs—Juvenile literature. I. Title.

   HV1569.6.B69 2011

   362.4'0483—dc22   2009033878

Printed in China

052010 Leo Paper Group, Heshan City, Guangdong, China.

10 9 8 7 6 5 4 3 2 1

To Our Readers: We have done our best to make sure all Internet Addresses in this book were active and appropriate when we went to press. However, the author and the publisher have no control over and assume n liability for the material available on those Internet sites or on other Web sites they may link to. Any comment or suggestions can be sent by e-mail to comments@enslow.com or to the address on the back cover.

Every effort has been made to locate all copyright holders of material used in this book. If any errors or omission have occurred, corrections will be made in future editions of this book.

Illustration Credits: Associated Press, pp. 16, 34, 40, 42, 45; Aurora/Getty Images, p. 37; Linda Bozz pp. 6, 8, 10, 12; Sae Hokoyama/Bergin University of Canine Studies, pp. 1, 3, 20, 27, 29, 31, 38; © To Nebbia/Corbis, p. 19; Shutterstock, pp. 22, 24; Victoria Yee/Getty Images, p. 44.

Cover Illustration: Sae Hokoyama/Bergin University of Canine Studies.

Contents

Thank You

Enslow Publishers, Inc. wishes to thank Krista Hardcastle-Utarid/Canine Companions for Independence for reviewing this book.

The author would like to thank Dr. Bonnie Bergin at the Assistance Dog Institute at the Bergin University of Canine Studies in Santa Rosa, California, for taking the time out from her busy schedule to share her memories and the history of service dogs.

Kazi

A True Story

"Sweater, get it," Jacqueline tells Kazi, her four-year-old golden retriever. Kazi wags his tail and trots over to where Jacqueline laid out her sweater the night before. He gently picks it up in his mouth and brings it to her. Kazi is not just any dog. He is Jacqueline's service dog.

Service dogs are trained to help people, like Jacqueline, who have physical disabilities. They help make people's lives easier. Jacqueline's disabilities

Jacqueline and her service dog Kazi.

involve the muscles in her body. These disabilities can make it painful for her to move at times. She also tires easily. "Kazi performs tasks for me throughout the day to help make my life easier," Jacqueline says.

When Jacqueline prepares breakfast, Kazi helps. He pulls out a pot and its lid, with his mouth, from the lower cabinet. This is helpful to Jacqueline, who finds it difficult to bend and even more difficult to get up. When it is time to leave for work, Kazi picks up Jacqueline's shoes, one at a time, in his mouth and brings them to her. On one particular morning, Jacqueline drops her keys on the floor. Even though Kazi is not in the room, he hears the keys hit the floor. He rushes in to help. Jacqueline rewards Kazi with lots of praise and his favorite treat.

Before Jacqueline and Kazi leave for work, Jacqueline slips Kazi's walker harness onto his back. A walker harness is a piece of equipment with a handle.

Kazi helps Jacqueline in the kitchen. He can open cabinet doors and get a lid.

Holding on to the handle helps Jacqueline walk. It also helps her to keep her balance.

When they arrive at the hospital where Jacqueline works, Kazi makes himself at home. He seems happy to stay with her in her office. He sits by her side during meetings. But when Jacqueline visits patients, Kazi rests in her office. It is there that he enjoys an afternoon nap.

At the end of Jacqueline's workday, it is time to head home. Kazi wags his tail as he helps Jacqueline walk safely back to her car. Each day, on their way home, they stop at the dog park. "Kazi must take a break from working. He needs to have some fun every day," Jacqueline explains. "He runs around the park for about thirty minutes."

Kazi helps Jacqueline in many ways. He serves as a brace if she needs help getting up. He is trained to open and close the refrigerator door by tugging

Kazi can even open the refrigerator door!

on a rope. He even brings Jacqueline his food dish when it is time for him to eat. "I'm always looking for new things to teach him to keep him interested," she says.

Most important, Kazi is quick to remind Jacqueline when she needs to rest. At the end of the day, Jacqueline's pain gets worse. She becomes very tired. "It is like he senses my pain." He follows Jacqueline around. This may be his way of telling her it is time take a break and rest. "Even when he can not help me physically, Kazi is by my side."

Before bed, Kazi gently pulls Jacqueline's socks off her feet. He tugs at her pants to help remove them. Finally, he gets her nightgown and brings it to her.

Having a service dog is helpful, but just like with any dog, it is also a lot of work. Jacqueline must keep Kazi groomed. This means brushing and combing his fur. She also brushes his teeth and clips his nails.

She must feed him and take him for walks. Jacqueline is responsible for taking Kazi to the veterinarian to keep him healthy. "Kazi takes care of me, and I take care of him. We are there for each other. Kazi and I are partners for life."

As a result of her physical disabilities, Jacqueline has good days and not so good days. What stays constant in her life is Kazi's love and his devotion to the work he performs. In Jacqueline's heart, Kazi is a true hero.

Chapter 1

The History of Service Dogs

Dogs have guided people with vision loss since the eighteenth century, or perhaps even earlier. The idea of dogs helping people with other physical disabilities came much later through the efforts of a woman named Dr. Bonnie Bergin.

It was in 1975 that Dr. Bergin founded Canine Companions for Independence, the first service dog program. This program trained and assisted in the placement of service dogs for people with physical disabilities.

Guide dogs help people who are blind live full lives.

During the 1970s, Dr. Bergin traveled to places like Asia, Australia, and Turkey as a high-school teacher. While in Turkey, Dr. Bergin often saw disabled people on the streets leaning on donkeys to help them walk. The donkeys also carried the goods that the people sold on the streets.

One day, Dr. Bergin saw something that stayed with her forever. A man with no use of his legs used his elbows to drag himself across a busy highway. "No one else seemed to notice, but I was shocked," Dr. Bergin recalled. Little did she know that this stranger would change her life.

When Dr. Bergin returned to the United States, she went back to school to learn about disabled people so she could teach them. It was during this time that she remembered the man crossing the busy street in Turkey. She remembered the people using donkeys to help them walk. Dr. Bergin knew donkeys would not be allowed to walk the streets in the United States, but she was sure dogs could because guide dogs were already doing it. "I knew this was the answer. I knew I just had to do it."

The first dog Dr. Bergin tried to train was a puppy of her own named Abdul. Abdul was a golden retriever and black Labrador retriever mix. "I had a dog, but I did not know anything about training them." Dr. Bergin used teaching skills that worked with her students to train the puppy in basic obedience. She then teamed up with a physically disabled person named Kerry Knaus, who was in a power wheelchair. Kerry told Dr. Bergin what kinds of tasks the dog would need to do to be able to help her. Dr. Bergin trained Abdul to turn on lights and pick things up for Kerry. Next, she trained Abdul to pull open the door to the house and the door to the refrigerator. Before long, he was getting Kerry's bagged lunch and putting

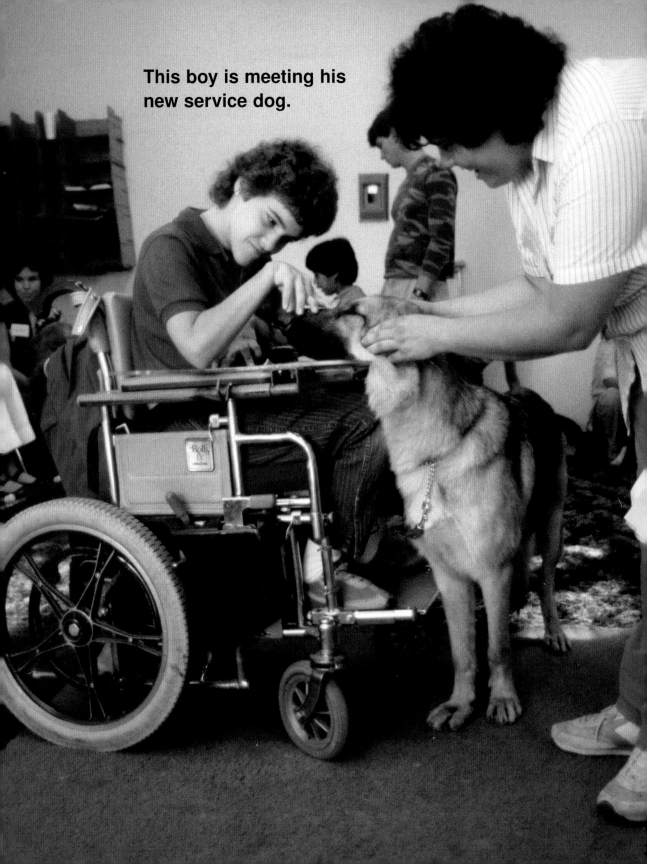

This boy is meeting his new service dog.

it on the tray in front of her. "I just kept adding more tasks," says Dr. Bergin. Kerry and Dr. Bergin continued to work together with Abdul, and the use of dogs for service was born.

Word of how Abdul helped Kerry quickly spread. Dr. Bergin began receiving requests for trained dogs. She adopted dogs from people and animal shelters before she learned to breed them herself for the

Service dogs help people with all kinds of disabilities.

qualities she needed. In just a year's time there was a wait list to receive one of Dr. Bergin's trained dogs.

In 1991, Dr. Bergin decided it was time to educate other people on how to start service dog programs. That is when she founded the Assistance Dog Institute at the Bergin University of Canine Studies in Santa Rosa, California. At the university, people learn to breed, train, and place service dogs with physically disabled people.

Dr. Bergin's work has shown people what dogs can do for physically disabled people. Many new training programs have been started based on the work she has done, while the need for service dogs continues to grow.

Dr. Bergin's hope for the future is that her students will discover new ways to improve on the work she has already done. "I tell my students, 'Go beyond today.'"

Labrador retrievers make good service dogs.

Chapter 2

Service Dog Breeds

Service dogs help people who are physically disabled to live more independent lives. This is an important job. Therefore, the type of dog should be carefully selected.

Service dogs and their partners work together as a team. It is best that the dog suits her partner and his or her needs.

Regardless of the breed, service dogs must be gentle and eager to work. They should be friendly and able to focus. That is why Labrador retrievers, golden retrievers, and a mix of the two are popular choices. German shepherds as well as other full and

German shepherds also make good service dogs.

mixed breeds have also been known to make good service dogs.

Service dogs need to be strong and able to help with tasks like pulling wheelchairs. Medium to large dogs can be used by people as a brace to help them stand or balance. Both male and female dogs make excellent service dogs.

Service dogs are often donated or purchased as puppies from breeders. Many successful service dogs are adopted by agencies from shelters, rescue groups, and even pet owners.

When choosing a service dog, the dog's personality traits are more important than the dog's breed or where the dog comes from. Service dogs and their partners work together as a team. It is best that the dog suits his partner's personality and physical needs.

Chapter 3

Service Dog Training

like other working dogs, service dogs need to be properly trained. Training guidelines may vary depending on the training program and the person's disability. The goal is the same, to prepare the service dog to assist a physically disabled person in living a more independent life.

Puppy Raiser

The puppy raiser's job is to prepare the puppy for skill training. This could take about eighteen months.

Most puppies will begin their training at just a few weeks old. Some programs prefer a puppy to start her training with a puppy raiser. A puppy raiser is usually a volunteer who provides a loving home while caring for the puppy. Together they attend classes to teach the dog basic obedience using simple commands. Commands may include sit, down, and stand, and many others.

Puppy trainers start training puppies when the puppies are just a few weeks old.

Service dogs spend much of their time working in public places. The puppy raiser and dog will visit places like malls and playgrounds to practice being in public. Service dogs must have good manners in public places. They need to be able to get along with people and other dogs.

Food is a popular reward when training dogs. Praise, playtime, and petting can also be successful training tools.

Skill Training

During skill training the dog learns to perform tasks related to the person's disability. So before skill training begins, dogs are matched with a recipient, the person receiving the dog. This way, the dog can be trained to meet her partner's specific needs. The dog will skill-train with a professional trainer who works for a service dog group.

Dogs are rewarded with treats, playtime, or a favorite toy after they have completed a task.

Among the skills taught are picking up dropped items, opening doors and drawers, and flipping switches for lights. In some cases, they may include pulling a wheelchair.

Team Training

Following skill training, the dog and the recipient train together as a team. During this time, they will get to know each other and hopefully begin to bond. The trainer watches to see that they are a good match.

At this time, the recipient, or handler, learns the

Service dogs are taken to local food stores. Once they are paired with a person, the dog will have to be able to safely travel to public places.

SERVICE DOG

IN TRAINING

commands that the dog has been taught. He or she will also learn how to take care of the dog, including feeding, watering, and grooming. Taking the dog for vaccinations and regular checkups with a veterinarian is also the recipient's responsibility.

Before bringing the dog home, the recipient must show that he or she can take care of the dog. The recipient must also demonstrate the ability to handle the dog in a safe manner. Finally, it is time for the recipient to bring the service dog home, where he or she will begin to live a more independent life with his or her new partner.

Chapter 4

Service Dogs on the Job

Service dogs have a special job. They help people with physical tasks. Some people are born with physical disabilities. Other disabilities may be a result of illness, injury, or aging. Service dogs perform tasks that help their disabled partners live more independent lives. Examples of disabilities:

- Arthritis
- Paraplegia
- Heart conditions
- Multiple sclerosis

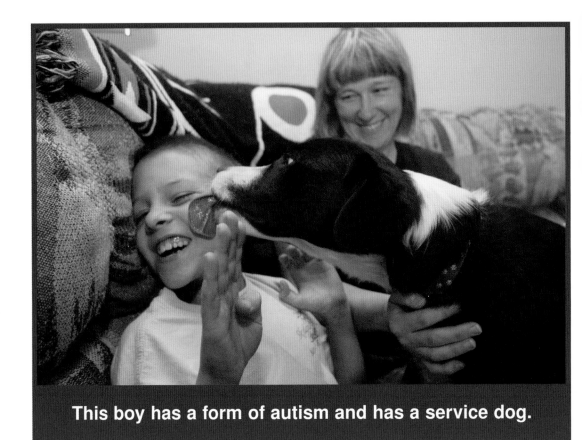

This boy has a form of autism and has a service dog.

Like all dogs, a service dog should wear a collar with a tag for identification. Most service dogs wear harnesses or vests with a patch when they work. This is so people will know that he is a service dog. The dog's partner keeps the dog on a leash in public in order to have full control of him. The handler may also carry an identification card that tells people the dog is a working service animal. It is okay to ask if you are not sure that the dog is a service dog.

Service dogs are working dogs. In public, they should never be petted without first asking if it is okay. Talking to or petting a service dog can keep her from doing her job. It is best to ignore a working service dog. But do not forget to say hello to the dog's human partner.

Service dogs are allowed in most public places where people are allowed. In public, a service dog should be clean and groomed. They should only go to the bathroom in places outdoors where dogs are supposed to go. A service dog should never bother or go after a person or another dog. They should never beg or take food from a public place. Service dogs should be quiet in public. That means no growling, whining, or barking if not necessary. Service dogs must always show good manners when in public places.

A service dog may help her partner shop during a trip to the mall. The dog may push an elevator button or pull her partner in a wheelchair up a ramp. The dog may also help pay and gather purchases when needed.

At home, the service dog continues working. The dog may help make dinner by opening the refrigerator door, opening a cabinet, or pulling out pots. The dog may also pick up dropped items as long as they are

Fast Fact

The Americans with Disabilities Act (ADA), which became law on July 26, 1990, provides public access for service dogs as a reasonable accommodation for a person with a disability.

This service dog is picking up the phone for the little girl.

Service dogs go anywhere their person needs to go. This service dog is taking a walk with his person.

not dangerous. These are just a few examples of the many tasks service dogs perform.

It is important for these hardworking dogs to have fun time, too. They love to play when they are not working. A game of fetch or just free running in a park provides exercise and a time for fun.

Chapter 5

When Service Dogs Retire

Like other working dogs, there comes a time when a service dog retires, or no longer works. When a dog retires may depend on the type of work the dog does. A dog that pulls a wheelchair will most likely retire before one that does not. Some dogs need to retire due to age or health problems.

Many people will go on a waiting list for a new dog before their current dog retires. This is so they will not have to go without help for a period of time.

It is often hard to retire a service dog, but what is best for the dog comes first.

Some people will choose to keep their retired service dog as a pet. Other times, service dogs may be returned to the group they came from, or they may be adopted into another loving home.

Being a part of a team is important for the service dog and person. The dog has to be able to get along with other dogs and people.

Fast Fact

Under the Americans with Disabilities Act (ADA), privately owned businesses that serve the public, such as restaurants, hotels, retail stores, taxicabs, theaters, concert halls, and sports facilities, are prohibited from discriminating against individuals with disabilities. The ADA requires these businesses to allow people with disabilities to bring their service animals onto business premises in whatever areas customers are generally allowed.

It is important to remember that each group and each dog is different. When service dogs finish their working careers, they have much to look forward to. After retirement they will continue to bring joy to many people. Most people would agree that this is the reward of a lifetime for these hardworking dogs.

Chapter 6

Service dogs are hardworking dogs that need time to play.

Service Dogs Are Heroes

Heroes make a difference in the lives of the people they help. That is why service dogs are heroes. They are able to change the lives of the people they help. Whether they are pulling a wheelchair or turning on a light switch, they are always there for their partners. A service dog and her partner work together as a team, taking care of each other. With hard work and love, this team shares many things, including a special bond. Service dogs make

Service dogs are a big help to those who need them.

better lives for the people who receive them. They open whole new worlds to people with disabilities. Service dogs enable people to do things they would not otherwise be able to do. With help from their dogs, disabled people are often able to work, travel, and even go to school. Service dogs are heroes that help make people's dreams come true!

A boy and his mother walk their service dog. Service dogs are truly heroes!

Glossary

brace—Something that supports weight.

breed—A certain type of dog.

breeders—People who raise certain types of dogs.

physical disabilities—Body conditions that may not allow people to do certain tasks.

trait—A quality that makes one dog different from another.

vaccinations—Shots that a dog needs to protect against illness.

veterinarian—A doctor who takes care of animals.

walker harness—A piece of equipment with a handle that service dogs sometimes wear.

Learn More

Books

Larrew, Brekka Hervey. *Labrador Retrievers.* Mankato, Minn.: Capstone Press, 2009.

Miller, Marie-Therese. *Helping Dogs.* New York: Chelsea Clubhouse, 2007.

O'Sullivan, Robyn. *More Than Man's Best Friend: The Story of Working Dogs.* Washington, D.C.: National Geographic, 2006.

Patent, Dorothy Hinshaw. *The Right Dog for the Job: Ira's Path from Service Dog to Guide Dog.* New York: Walker & Company, 2004.

Internet Addresses

American Humane Association
  <http://www.americanhumane.org>

American Kennel Club: Kids' Corner
  <http://www.akc.org/public_education/kids_
    corner/kidscorner.cfm>

Index